WORSHIP

Creating opportunities to meet and respond to God

By Daniel T. Benedict, Jr.
General Board of Discipleship

WORSHIP

Copyright © 2004 by Cokesbury

This book is printed on acid-free paper.

ISBN 0-687-03669-0

MANUFACTURED IN THE UNITED STATES OF AMERICA

CONTENTS

Our Identity, Call, and Mission

You are so important to the life of the Christian church! You have consented to be among a great and long line of people who have shared the faith and led others in the work of Jesus Christ. We have the church only because over the millennia people like you have caught the vision of God's kingdom and have claimed a place in the faith community to extend God's love to others. You have been called and have committed your unique passions, gifts, and abilities in a position of leadership, and this guide will help you understand some of the elements of that ministry and how it fits within the mission of your church and of The United Methodist Church.

"The mission of the Church is to make disciples of Jesus Christ. Local churches provide the most significant arena through which disciple-making occurs" (*The Book of Discipline of The United Methodist Church, 2004,* ¶120). The church is not only local but also global, and it is for everyone. Our church has an organizational structure through which we work, but it is a living organism as well. Each person is called to ministry by virtue of his or her baptism, and that ministry takes place in all aspects of daily life, not just within the walls of the church. Our *Book of Discipline* describes our mission to proclaim the gospel and to welcome people into the body of Christ, to lead people to a commitment to God through Jesus Christ, to nurture them in Christian living by various means of grace, and to send them into the world as agents of Jesus Christ (¶121). Thus, through you—and many other Christians—this very relational mission continues. (The *Discipline* explains the ministry of all Christians and the essence of servant ministry and leadership in ¶¶125–137.)

Essential Leadership Functions

Five functions of leadership are essential to strengthen and support the ministry of the church: identifying and supporting leaders as spiritual leaders, discovering current reality, naming shared vision, developing action plans, and monitoring the journey. This Guideline will help you identify these elements and set a course for ministry.

Lead in the Spirit

Each leader is a spiritual leader and has the opportunity to model spiritual maturity and discipline. John Wesley referred to the disciplines that cultivate a relationship with God as the "means of grace" and suggested several means: prayer, Bible study, fasting, public and private worship, Christian conversation, and acts of mercy. Local church leaders are strongly encouraged to identify their own spiritual practices, cultivate new ones as they grow in their own faith, and model and encourage these practices among their ministry team participants.

Discover Current Reality

"The way things are" is your current reality. How you organize, who does what, how bills get paid and plans get made are all building blocks of your current reality. Spend time with people who have been in this ministry and with your committee and/or other leaders to assess their view of how things are. Use "Christian conversation," one of the means of grace, not only to talk to others openly about their understanding of current reality but also to listen for the voice of God regarding your area of ministry.

Name Shared Vision

"The way things are" is only a prelude to "the way you want things to be." When the church is truly of God, it is the way God would envision it to be. Spend time with your committee and with other leaders in the church to discern the best and most faithful future you can imagine. How can you together identify your role and place in a faithful community that extends itself in its fourfold mission of reaching out and receiving people in the name of God, relating people to God, nurturing them in Christ and Christian living, and sending them forth as ministers into the world? Examine your committee's role and its place in that big picture and try to see yourselves as God's agents of grace and love.

Develop Action Plans

How do you get from here (your current reality) to there (your shared vision)? As a leader, one of your tasks is to hold in view both what is and what is hoped for so that you can build bridges to the future. These bridges are the interim goals and the action plans needed to accomplish the goals that will make your vision a reality. Remember that God may open up many (or different) avenues to that future, so be flexible and open to setting new goals and accepting new challenges. Action plans that describe how to meet interim goals should be specific, measurable, and attainable. While it is faithful to allow for the wondrous work of God in setting out bold plans, balance that boldness with realism. You and your committee will find information and tips here on developing and implementing the shared vision, the goals toward that vision, and the specific action plans that will accomplish the goals.

Monitor the Journey

A fifth responsibility of leaders is to keep an eye on how things are going. Setbacks will surely occur, but effective leaders keep moving toward their envisioned future. Not only will you monitor the progress of your action plans to a faithful future but you will also be called to evaluate them in light of the ministry of the rest of the church. Immerse yourself and your plans in God's love and care. Voices from the congregation (both pro and con) may be the nudging of God to shift direction, rethink or plan, or move ahead boldly and without fear. Faithful leaders are attentive to the discernment of the congregation and to the heart of God in fulfilling the mission of the church.

Getting Started

What Is My Job?

You will work with your pastor and music leader(s) to ensure that your congregation provides opportunities for worship that will help the congregation experience its relationship with God and will help it live more faithfully as a Christian community. You will work closely with the church council to respond to God's call. In short, your job is to help your church offer settings for vital worship in which people experience the presence of God and grow in the knowledge of God.

What Are My Basic Responsibilities?

1. To learn about worship and about people in your congregation and community so you can plan worship appropriate to their needs.
2. To collaborate with the pastor and music leaders in planning worship.
3. To develop and support effective musical leadership in the church.
4. To promote and foster regular individual and family spiritual formation.
5. To consider other opportunities for strengthening worship (see pages 24-26).

What Does the Chairperson Do?

You will find more detail on each of these on pages 13-26.
1. Stay in communication with the pastor and music leader(s).
2. Guide the work of the worship ministry group through the year, and if there is a worship committee (work area), plan its agendas and preside at its meetings.
3. Plan worship (at least quarterly) with the pastor, music leader(s), and others who may be responsible for planning and leading worship. This cooperative planning, led by the pastor, should outline all worship services, including Scriptures, music, and any special services.
4. Consult with and support the music leader(s) in your congregation.
5. Promote the spiritual life of your congregation and all of its members.
6. Participate, if appropriate to your congregation's structure, in the church council (council on ministries and administrative board) and charge conference representing the concerns of worship.
7. Discover the literature and other resources available that are related to worship and share them with other worship leaders.
8. Participate in training events that are related to worship.

Quick Start Tips

1. **Meet with the pastor** to discover her or his concerns about worship. Discover how you can best collaborate in shaping worship that strengthens congregational life and faithful discipleship.

2. **Talk with the person who previously served** in the position you now hold. Ask: "What is important for me to know as I begin to lead? Are there plans that I need to carry out?"

3. **Convene a meeting of the worship ministry committee** (if organized) or meet with other key people with worship-related responsibilities to evaluate and plan for the year. Meet within thirty days of your election. Talk about mutual expectations, hopes, and values related to your congregation and its worship opportunities. Discuss and decide what your group or committee will do in the coming year. Decide how often to meet and set the dates for the year.

4. **Plan the agenda for the coming meetings.** Look at the calendar in light of seasons and special services (Advent, Christmas, Lent, Easter) and decide how far in advance you and others will need to plan.

5. **Consider the worship hopes and concerns** of people in your congregation and community. Ask questions. Listen.

6. **Explore and become familiar with the primary worship books** and resources used in your congregation, particularly *The United Methodist Hymnal* and *The United Methodist Book of Worship*, especially the opening sections on the basic pattern and related orders.

7. **Evaluate your congregation's worship.** What is working well? How could it be improved? Is worship in your church grounded in the best of the Christian tradition? Is it relevant to the culture and setting of your people and your community?

8. **Talk with people who have (or have had) responsibilities similar to yours.** These persons may be in your congregation or in other congregations.

9. **Participate in training events.** Ask your pastor, district superintendent, and conference program staff what events they know about. Make sure that the secretarial staff gives you information about these events. Ask if there are funds to assist you in attending.

You are being asked to see the whole experience of worship. You are being asked to help the pastor and the musicians to hear what the congregation is saying and feeling.

Help Is Available

K now that you are not alone in your work. You have powerful allies and terrific supporters. The Spirit will work in you as you use the spiritual disciplines of prayer, Scripture reflection, worship, and share with other Christians:

- the pastor
- the musician(s)
- the person who served in your role before you
- your district or annual conference's elected worship person
- your annual conference program staff
- the worship staff of the General Board of Discipleship
- a feast of good books, magazines, Web sites, seminars, workshops, and videotapes
- organizations committed to strengthening worship, such as the Fellowship of United Methodists in Music and Worship Arts and the Order of Saint Luke.

You will find more information about the last three bulleted items in the Resources at the end of this Guideline. The main thing to realize is that you have ready support and assistance. The next move is yours: ASK, SEEK, KNOCK! (Matthew 7:7-11).

But before you zip off to do all that, let's take a little time to get a picture of worship in your church—not just how it is, but how it could be by the power of the Spirit. Then we will get to doing the things that will move toward making that picture a reality.

First, Pray and Listen

Prayer and listening are basic components of spiritual leadership. Let's experience prayer as listening. Set aside some time to listen to God. If now is not the time, choose a time and place when you can be comfortable and at ease. Have pen and paper available. Read one or two passages in the Bible that evoke a sense of the power and presence of God. Here are some suggested selections: Psalm 148; Isaiah 6:1-8; 1 Peter 2:4-10; Revelation 4:1-11. Now relax and close your eyes, breathing deeply and exhaling a few times. *Think of a favorite place of peace and rest and imagine being in that place.* Give yourself time to "be" in that place.

Next, recall a time when you experienced worship and the presence of God. Maybe it was a long time ago. Maybe it was in a recent service.

Take a few minutes to reenter that experience. When you are ready, thank God for that time and for what you sensed of God's love, nearness, power, grace, mercy, and call.

Worship is not so much about us as it is about God.

When you are ready to move on, recall what you remember about how others experienced that moment. Maybe they experienced what you did. Maybe most missed what you experienced. Either way it is all right. List in your thoughts or on paper the factors that made the moment a deep and powerful experience for you (and for others if they, too, felt the power of that moment).

Next, recall the result or impact of that moment in your life. Did you see something differently or gain insight? Did you make a commitment to do something you sensed God asking you to do? Was something consoled that was aching, or was something made whole that was broken? Did some part of you that was angry or resentful become peaceful and centered?

Now, take time to ask: "Lord, what are my deepest longings for others who participate in worship in our church?" (You probably need to start with that question so your own longings can move out of the way in listening to God and others.) Then ask, "God, what is it that you want people to do and experience in worship? What is my pastor's vision for worship? What is the vision of the music leader(s)? What do the people long for?" Imagine people who live in the community around your church building. What do they long for in relationship to God? Do they even know God? How could worship say to them, "You are welcome to be here and to come as you are with whatever longings and questions you have"? Listen to what you sense coming back toward you as you ask these questions. Attend to what God is saying to you. When you are ready to break from this inward journey, thank God for this time and hear God's blessing on you and an invitation to come and listen again. Then as a way of exiting from the inward space, say the Lord's Prayer aloud softly.

This exercise in prayer and listening is a way to begin shaping your vision for worship in your congregation. What you now see is not all there is to see, but it gives you a place to begin in conversations that you have with other leaders. *You are a person who shares in the "great congregation" (Psalm 22:25) and who has a history and experience before the Holy One of Israel.*

Second, Think About

What Makes Worship Vital?

The worship services of your congregation are meant to be alive and vital with God's presence and the people's participation—God calling, the people responding. When worship is alive, *you know it*! When it is not, *you know that too*.

Vital or lifeless? Full or empty? *What* makes the difference? *Who* in your church can help make the difference? The following pages are designed to assist you in planning vital worship in your congregation. You are one of the many people who participate in making worship what it is and *what it can be*.

Whether your congregation is large or small, rural, small town, or big city, you know when worship is vital. There is energy in what happens. The power of God's Word touches the hurts and awakens the hopes of real people. Visitors are glad they came. People participate because the singing, the hearing, the praying, the sharing at the table, and the sending people out are done in ways that say, "This matters." In vital worship the people are addressed, touched, washed, fed, anointed, and strengthened in relationship to God and to one another.

In the following pages you will find invitations for conversation and reflection about worship. You may not want to read this from cover to cover; maybe you will find yourself going to the places that seem to address what you really want to know now. Feel free to skip around and come back to things as you need them. *The main thing is that you discover a passion for helping worship become more faithful and vital in your congregation and that you sense you are a leader equipped with resources.* You are a member of the team with a unique job to do.

What Does Vital Worship Look, Feel, Smell, Taste, and Sound Like?

- People are welcomed, honored, and cared for.
- God's story, which is our story, is always told.
- Jesus is experienced as present in love and power.
- The people and the community are changed by the power of the Holy Spirit.
- People are active in singing, praying, and responding.
- There is passion in the singing, preaching, and praying.
- Varied ages and cultures are welcomed.
- Things (food, water, candles, furnishings, fabrics, vessels) are used generously to point to the presence of God.
- Actions (people being baptized, greeting one another, sharing bread and cup) point to the presence of the risen Lord.
- Worship space is arranged so the people can be together and see one another.
- There are calls and responses: people experience God calling, and they respond.

- Leaders work in concert to prompt the participation of all the people.
- Leaders are prepared to and expectant of hearing God's Word and experiencing God's power.
- Leaders act with the people.
- Everyone acts in ways that say, "Worship matters."
- People who are experiencing hurt and isolation receive a healing touch.
- People's hope is awakened.
- All the people have a sense of belonging and know how to participate.
- People are free to observe when they need to watch and listen as a way of preparing to participate more fully.
- There is energy, and the way worship unfolds makes sense.
- The worship reveals the planning, gifts, and preparation of the people.

You may think of other experiences. What are they?

Why Does Vitality in Worship Matter?

Worship matters because people are seeking God. Perhaps the searching is more evident in people outside the church than inside it. Browse the best sellers that people are reading. Look at the growing number of twelve-step groups and New Age religious expressions. People are searching for something real, spiritual, and powerful. People are longing for meaning, belonging, and something or someone to live for.

With other leaders in your congregation, ask the following questions.
- Who are we?
- How do we enact our search for God? How does worship invite us to express the longings we have?
- Are our people willing to welcome others who are searching to be active participants in worship?
- Where in worship are we most alive to God and to one another? How could we improve?

Who Is Worship For?

Is worship for God? For church members? For those who are not now part of your church? Certainly worship is about honoring and praising God. That is the meaning of the word. Keep this focus on God in view.

Hospitality and welcome are essential to Christian worship, whatever the style. Many churches are implementing services characterized as "seeker-friendly" or "contemporary worship." This booklet will not attempt to describe or advocate these variations on the services outlined in our hymnals and book of worship. If you would like more information and guidance about such services, see the Resources section at the end of this booklet or visit the worship Web site: www.umcworship.org.

And you may be thinking, "Isn't worship *for the people* who already belong to the church? Yes, worship to God is offered by a particular community of people. Worship is never generic or a commodity to be consumed. Its context is always a particular group of believers who gather regularly and offer "their" unique gifts and energies to God. You may also be thinking, *"But what about those who are not yet part of the church?"* Exactly! The Scriptures from the beginning are clear that God's people exist to be a light to the nations (Genesis 12:1-3; Isaiah 42:6-7; Luke 2: 29-32). For the moment, think of it this way: If the congregation's essential work is to do everything in such a way that people are welcomed, changed by God's story and presence, and sent out to love and serve in daily life, then worship is for all people. Worship is for everyone who longs for God—believers and seekers. In this, God is honored and served.

Christian worship is our public work as Christians. The door needs to be open—*wide open*—so that all people will know they are welcome to explore and search and discover the good news in Jesus Christ.

Who Are the People Not Now Part of Your Worship?

- Children
- Youth
- Baby boomers, generation X, millennials
- People of a racial/ethnic group different from most of your congregation
- People with mental or physical disabilities

Can you identify others?

What Vision Moves You?

Vital worship is part of the flow of people *gathering to celebrate* the good news and then *scattering to live* the good news in everyday relationships. When worship is not vital, that flow becomes constricted like a plugged pipe. When music is lifeless or preaching is irrelevant to people's yearnings and struggles, the risen Christ seems less with us. When baptism and Communion are mere ceremonies instead of powerful moments of connection with the living Lord and with one another, worship wilts.

You may be wondering, *"Is lively, flowing worship about hand clapping and shouting 'Alleluia'? Is it stained glass, silence, and pipe organs?"* The style and technologies used can be varied, depending on the setting. The basic structure of worship (gathering, Word, Communion and sending forth—see the *Hymnal* p. 2) accommodates our human diversity. As you lead in the search for vital worship in your setting, you will discover the uniqueness of how your congregation tells and celebrates the Christian story.

What Can You Do to Lead Toward Vital Worship?

Stay in Communication With the Worship Leaders

The pastor and musicians lead worship from week to week. In some churches there is a team of persons who meet every week to plan worship for the coming Sunday and for the services several weeks from that point. Your pastor and congregation may use the lectionary and the calendar of the Christian year (see *The Book of Worship*, pages 227-237) as a primary tool for planning. They may use some other plan. In any case, you will need to get in step with these planners and gain a sense of the rhythms and patterns of their work, the decisions they make, and the way they conceive worship Sunday by Sunday and season by season. No two pastors plan the same way. Similarly, no two music leaders prepare the same way. As a first step, invite them to show you how they go about it.

Once you have a sense of their planning approach, ask if there is a way that you could support them, and find the ways in which they are open to additional minds and hands sharing the work of preparing for worship.

Then develop your own patterns for planning and preparation. Maybe you will meet monthly with the pastor to check in and see if she has any thoughts on how it's going. Maybe you will make a point to affirm the music ministry each Sunday and ask if there is anything you can do to support the work of the choir or the accompanist. Sometimes, you will lead by listening. If you sense there is an openness to talk, find the time and place.

Guide the Worship Ministry Group

You are responsible for guiding the work of the congregation with respect to worship. You don't manage the day-to-day affairs of worship. Others do that, but you represent the members' interests and their concerns to the pastor and staff, and you are knowledgeable about the ways the pastor and staff do the work entrusted to them.

You call the meetings of the staff and the worship team (leader of ushers, acolyte leader, greeter coordinator, and some people from the congregation who are interested or called to care about worship even though they may not have a particular worship-related task). You plan the agenda in consultation with the pastor and other worship staff. You consider the needs and expressions of the people in setting the agenda.

You also plan the agenda by keeping in mind that worship is not what the pastor and staff do; rather, it is the work of the people who offer themselves "in praise and thanksgiving as a holy and living sacrifice, in union with Christ's offering for us." (See "The Great Thanksgiving" on page 10 of the *Hymnal* and Romans 12:1.) Sometimes your work will be to ensure that the conversation of the meeting will focus on the work of the people as primary, while the work of the pastor and musicians is to preside and guide the people's work.

Here is an example of a worship meeting agenda with specific suggestions on the opposite page. Plan to meet at least four times each year. You will have to adapt the agenda to the needs and realities of your congregation. If your congregation is large and its worship life complex, you may need to meet more often.

Sample Agenda
(Have Bibles and hymnals for each person.)
1. **Scripture reflection and prayer**. Read the text twice, asking after the first time, "What word or image stands out for you?" After the second time, ask, "What invitation is here for us as a worshiping community?" Allow for silence after asking the questions. Close with prayer, perhaps using one of the prayers in the *Hymnal*. (See the titles in italics in the index of the *Hymnal*, pages 934-954.)
2. **Reflection on worship experience**. Ask, "What is going well? What needs to be improved?"
3. **Long-range planning**. Here bring up or report on any long-range changes contemplated.
4. **Seasonal planning.** Use the *Book of Worship* for orientation and reflection on the coming liturgical season. (Pass out copies of the *Book of Worship* with book markers inserted at key pages. You can use these as tools for orientation and reflection. You or the pastor could highlight the main seasonal themes. The book gives you permission to make copies if you need to.)
● The pastor shares his or her direction in preaching and worship for the approaching season. Musicians may also want to share plans. (Invite them to prepare for this ahead of time.)

● What special services will we schedule?

● What changes do we want to make in the seasonal worship this year?

● What special tasks need to be assigned? to whom?

● How will we make special services known in the church and community?

5. **Short-range planning.** What "incidental" or occasional issues may need special attention?

Specific Agenda Suggestions

1. Scripture for Reflection
   Winter meeting: Luke 19:29-40
   Spring meeting: Luke 24:13-35
   Summer meeting: Revelation 4:1-11 (also hymns "Majesty" (176), "Holy, Holy, Holy" (64), or another hymn of high praise and adoration before reading
   Fall meeting: Isaiah 2:1-4

3. Long-Range Planning Suggestions (as relevant)
   Redesign of the chancel space; frequency of Communion; adding a service; introduction of new instrumentation; and training acolytes, readers, and Communion servers

4. Seasonal Planning
   Winter meeting: (to plan for Lent and Easter; roughly the months of February to May) See *Book of Worship* pages 224, 320, and 368.
   Suggested special services: Ash Wednesday, Holy Thursday, Good Friday, Easter Vigil, Baptism, Confirmation.

Spring Meeting: (to plan for the Great Fifty Days, Trinity Sunday, Pentecost, and the early months of Ordinary Time; roughly the months of April to August) See *Book of Worship* pages 224 and 409. Will there be any changes for summer?

Summer meeting: (to plan for the latter part of Ordinary Time; roughly September through November) See *Book of Worship* pages 224 and 409.

Fall meeting: (to plan for the final weeks of Ordinary Time, Thanksgiving, Christ the King, Advent, and Christmas) See *Book of Worship* pages 224, 238, 269, and 409.

5. Short-Range Planning Items (as needed)
   Piano tuning; scheduling readers, liturgists, ushers, greeters, Communion servers for the next three months; supplies available (candles, Communion items, flowers, and so on); sound system maintenance; attention to hospitality and welcoming; accurate and inviting publicity and advertising.

Plan Worship at Least Quarterly

This cooperative planning, with others who are responsible for worship, led by the pastor, should outline all worship services, including Scriptures, music, and any special services.

You may think that was discussed in the section above. That was the "big picture" planning. *This is about detailed planning for every service.* Although your worship planners may not use a chart such as "A Worksheet for Planning a Worship Service" (p. 27), it gives you some idea of the kind of detail that needs to be planned for each service. Feel free to copy or adapt the chart to your congregation's weekly planning needs. Keep a notebook with a planning page for every service for the year in it and fill it in as you go. (This may not work or be necessary in every church.)

There is no single way to plan worship, but many churches are discovering that cooperative worship planning is more satisfying over time than "flying solo" planning. The way in which you and other leaders become part of cooperative worship planning will vary depending on the size, location, traditions, and leadership patterns in your local congregation. Here are several ways you may choose to plan.

Use a planning guide to measure where you are now and periodically to measure your improvement. The main thing here is to discover how much more alive worship can become when you plan together. *Note: weddings and funerals are occasions for a different kind of team planning.* The individuals or families involved can be seen as part of a team with the pastor and church musician. They bring important knowledge and feelings to the planning work leading to the wedding or funeral.

Plan together, trusting that you will find enjoyment and creativity in the process. In some instances, the pastor decides on the Scripture passages and title for next Sunday's sermon and lists the hymns and prayers for the bulletin. (This is often done in very small churches or in settings without an active worship team or professional music leader.) In other situations, the pastor sets out the texts and themes for the sermons several weeks or months ahead and passes them along to the musician or secretary to "fill in the blanks" for the rest of the service. (This can happen where the preacher does the planning several months ahead, focusing on sermon more than on the rest of the worship service.) Or, the pastor, worship chairperson, and music leader meet to consider the focus, text, and flow of a particular worship service with the aid of Bible study, dialogue, and sharing of mutual gifts. (This process can involve both lay and clergy in a regularly scheduled meeting.)

Talk to the pastor and other worship leaders about how you could expand and improve your cooperative worship planning capacity. Meet frequently enough to engage the best gifts and most creative thinking and planning from all participants.

Improving Worship: The Quality Questions

Your church may be frightened of change. *You* may be frightened of change. Maybe you remember times when someone tried to change the worship and frustration, unhappiness, and anger resulted. Of course! Worship is important. The symbols and values of our lives are at stake!

There is another way. *People who agree to work and plan together can ask some very basic questions that we call the "quality questions."*

- What went well today?
- What could be improved?
- What did we learn?

Imagine your worship leaders getting together every week to ask those questions. Each might have different answers to each question. That is okay. List all the answers. Some might be the same for one or more of you. That means you have some shared sense of what worked well or of what could be improved. Maybe you will discover that a hymn new to the congregation seems to drain the energy from the service. Does that mean you should not try new hymns or songs? Or does it mean your team needs to try some better ways to teach or use a new hymn or song?

The quality improvement questions let you and others make gradual but continuous improvement in your congregation's worship.

Work With the Music Leader(s)

We've been called the "Singing Methodists" because from the early days of the Methodist movement, song has been a primary way of celebrating and proclaiming our faith and offering our prayer.

Music accounts for at least 40 percent of the impact of a worship service. The pastor of one of our fastest growing United Methodist congregations, when asked for his "secret," said, "First music, then preaching, in that order." The music in your worship service may determine whether visitors return to your church and whether members feel that they have participated and been nurtured. Whether your congregation cherishes traditional sacred music "classics," rocks to contemporary praise and worship choruses, or enjoys a variety of musical styles, *the quality and content of the music in worship will in large measure determine the vitality of the overall experience of the people. In other words, music and congregational song are important.*

The musical players are the congregation, perhaps a director of music, the choir(s), accompanist(s), vocal and instrumental soloists, the pastor, and you. *Yours is a crucial role because you are called to see the whole picture and consult and collaborate with the leaders in ways that music and music leaders maximize their contribution to the praise of God and the response of the people.*

Here are some of your responsibilities in consulting with and supporting music leaders.
● Recognize, encourage, and nurture musicians in your congregation, both volunteer and paid.
● Work with musicians, pastor, and your staff/pastor-parish relations committee to establish clear job descriptions.
● Work with the musicians and pastor in preparing a clear vision and mission statement for your church's music ministry. Be sure that it reflects a shared understanding of congregational song and worship in fulfilling the primary task of the church and its vision for the future.
● Develop with the musicians and pastor an intentional plan for teaching people of all ages our heritage in song and the joy of congregational singing.
● See that an adequate budget for music is a priority for the congregation, including appropriate compensation for paid musicians, provisions for new music and instruments and their upkeep, continuing education funds, and funding for special seasonal needs.
● Develop a long-range process for discovering and training people in your congregation and community who can become tomorrow's church musicians. This should include opportunities for children and youth in worship and in choirs and other music experiences.

Copyright and Licensing Information

In a media-oriented age with photocopiers, VCRs, LCD projectors, and other high-tech equipment, more and more churches are finding ways to use music and projected visuals in the context of worship. There are serious ethical and legal questions involved in this use. *You need to be aware of these issues and encourage other leaders to use legal means in employing music, video, and DVDs with copyright restrictions.*

Music

The Copyright Act of 1976 prohibits the unauthorized reproduction of copyrighted materials including song sheets, overhead transparencies, bulletin inserts, slides, and LCD (liquid crystal display) projection. **Churches are not exempt from this law.** Permission to use some copyrighted material may be secured from organizations that have received licensing rights from various music publishers. These services allow congregations who subscribe the right to reprint texts and music (in the form of song sheets, bulletin inserts, transparencies, LCD projection, and/or slides) from a variety of, but not all, publishers. Fees are based on average worship attendance. Some record keeping is required.

● **Christian Copyright Licensing, Inc. (CCLI)**
17201 N.E. Sacramento St.
Portland, Oregon 97230
Telephone: 800-234-2446 or 503-257-2230
Fax: 503-257-2244
Website: www.ccli.com
CCLI has the largest number of publishers, including: some United Methodist publishing groups, Word, Hope, Maranatha!, and Integrity Hosanna. Most praise choruses are covered by a CCLI license. **The CCLI license never covers G.I.A. publications.**

● **LicenSing**
Logos Production
6160 Carmen Avenue East
Inver Grove Heights, Minnesota 55076-4422
Telephone: 651-451-9945
Fax: 651-457-4617
Website: www.joinhands.com
LicenSing covers a smaller list of publishers and is designed more for mainline, liturgical congregations or for churches that use traditional music. It includes some United Methodist publishing groups, more international companies, and overlaps some of the same publishers covered by CCLI. **The LicenSing license never covers G.I.A. publications.**

● **G.I.A. Publications, Inc.**
7404 South Mason Avenue
Chicago, Illinois 60638-9927
Telephone: 800-442-1358 or 708-496-3800
Fax: 708-496-3828
Web site: www.giamusic.com

G.I.A. provides a wide range of music resources including music from Taizé, Iona, Scripture, and liturgical songs. G.I.A. licenses churches to use its music resources under specific regulations. **The G.I.A. license never covers music covered by the CCLI or LicenSing licenses.**

Movies and Videos

Similar copyright restrictions apply to video formats of films. The opening words of commercial videos indicate that the tape or DVD is intended for "home use only." Legally, this excludes use in churches, either for worship or for educational and entertainment settings, such as youth fellowship or child care. As with the music licensing companies, you may purchase a license that will allow you to show videos legally of some popular films in your church. The license will allow you to show a video in its entirety, or scenes from a video, but not to edit it in any way. Modest fees are based on the anticipated viewing audience.

● **Christian Video Licensing International (CVLI)**
Licensing Office
17201 NE Sacramento Street
Portland, Oregon 97230
Telephone: 888-335-4844
Fax: 503-257-2244
Website: www.cvli.org

In some annual conferences, the conference media center holds a license for the use of video resources. Check with your annual conference media center.

Promote Spiritual Life

Our Methodist heritage is strongly oriented to the means of grace (prayer, Holy Communion, Scripture and devotional reading, participation in public worship, preaching, fasting, Christian conversation, and so on). In your church there may be specific persons, including the pastor, who focus their attention on forming habits that deepen discipleship in all of the people. Whether that is true in your situation, your attention to worship is clearly linked to that concern. Through your worship group and church council, promote the spiritual life of all members of the congregation using these resources and actions.

Celebrate God's story every week using the lectionary and the Christian calendar. Good worship forms faith by rehearsing God's story. The calendar and lectionary aim at making and forming Christians.

See and affirm the connections between worship and everyday life. People long for the affirmation that their lives matter and that God is at work in their jobs, family life, leisure activities, friendships, and community involvement. In sermons, worship, and small groups, affirm the connections between faith and life.

Invite the people to read the Scriptures for worship during the week. Publish the Sunday readings in advance and encourage all the people to read and reflect on them during the week. In this way all of the people become partners in preaching and are prepared worship participants.

Offer small groups for prayer, Bible study, and mutual accountability for discipleship. Christian faith is not a go-it-alone experience. A basic ingredient of effective discipleship is participation in small groups where people can experience what John Wesley described as "watching over each other in love." Growing churches offer a variety of small groups.

Provide and encourage the use of *The Upper Room* and *The Upper Room Disciplines.* Help people with private prayer and daily reflection on Scripture by promoting the use of daily devotional books available through the Upper Room. (See the Resources section at the end of this booklet.)

Introduce and offer prayer for healing. Many people have a great need for Jesus' healing touch. In special services or in the context of regular worship, use the healing services in the *Book of Worship* to offer prayer for healing to anyone who seeks it. Teach about healing using the *Book of Worship*'s introduction to those services. Include stations for healing prayer in each communion service.

Call people to a continuing conversion and renewal of the baptismal covenant. In baptism we are called to a lifelong journey of resisting evil and trusting Christ. Advent and Lent in particular are times of stirring our faith toward repentance and renewal. Plan services of renewal of the baptismal covenant on the Baptism of the Lord, Easter, Pentecost, and other appropriate days. (See Baptismal Covenant I and IV in the *Hymnal*.) If your congregation has revivals, relate the revivals to the baptismal covenant. Invite seekers into a journey toward baptism or renewal of the baptismal covenant.

Call seekers and newcomers to a life of faith. Encourage the pastor to make sermons invitational. Offer seekers an opportunity to explore their questions, tell their stories, and learn the good news in Jesus Christ. Make faith-sharing the work of the whole congregation. Appoint sponsors to partner with seekers. Let them mentor seekers in learning to worship, pray, reflect on Scripture, and serve God and neighbor in daily life. Do more than make church members—pray for Christ to call disciples. *Come to the Waters* by Daniel Benedict proposes a bold model for inviting people to a conversion journey.

Participate in the Church Council and Charge Conference

Your church's ministry of reaching out to people, relating them to God, nurturing them in the faith, and sending them out to live as disciples in the community and world is guided by the church council. (In some congregations it is called the council on ministries or the administrative council.) This group is a council of leaders who share a vision of the congregation's service to God in welcoming people, forming, and supporting them in a life of discipleship in daily living. You are a part of that council of spiritual leaders.

Your participation is crucial. On the one hand, you are not there merely to promote the cause of worship; you share in the concern of the leaders for the whole range of ministries aimed at making disciples and at ordering the life of the congregation around the means of grace. On the other hand, the council will depend on you to be a voice of authority and passion for the centrality of worship in the congregation's life. Worship is a distinctive and formative action of the congregation. It is crucial to the flow of the church's life.

You participate in the council to see that the whole primary task of the congregation is working. You lead by asking questions and by envisioning how worship relates to the rest of the flow that seeks God's grace to work transforming love and justice in every person and in the whole congregation.

The charge conference is another setting for your participation and leadership. The United Methodist Church works by a series of "conferences." These conferences are understood as the settings for discerning God's will and holding the church accountable for its work in the name of God. For example, the General Conference is the worldwide conference and is responsible for the work of the whole church globally. The annual conference is a regional conference, sometimes corresponding to the boundaries of a state. The charge conference is the local church (sometimes, several churches together) and is responsible for embodying locally Christ's ministry of making disciples. The General Conference and annual conference exist to support and provide resources for this local ministry. The charge (local) conference reviews and evaluates the total ministry of the congregation, sets goals, and elects leaders to carry out the work. You will be asked to make a worship report at the meeting or to share in a group report on worship as one of the ministries of the congregation.

If You Have Trouble

Sometimes, there is friction in relationships. Perhaps the pastor is jealous of anyone who tries to make suggestions or take initiative. Sometimes a musician seems unwilling or too busy to sit down for a meeting. In some cases the congregation does not want to consider changes that would make the worship more accessible to children or to people in the neighborhood. You have a choice to make: give up or love.

● Recognize that if you choose to love, you won't give up; and you will find an open door when it appears that all of them are closed. If you love, you can talk to the person or persons who are resistant. Listen. See if you can see what they see and feel what they are afraid of.

● Realize that you don't have to "have it your way" right now. It isn't your way that counts as much as it is that you have a vision of something that others may not be able to see. Find out who else shares your vision. Talk with them. Find a way to share the vision with others. Discover where the resistance is. Explore ways to address that resistance.

● Be sure the pastor is supportive of you. It is not the pastor's church, but the pastor is charged with oversight of worship. Your job is always to work with your pastor. That is a tall order and sometimes a very difficult pathway. Walk the pathway in love and prayer.

● If you really get stuck, talk with the appropriate people. If it is a staff member with whom you get stuck, talk with your staff/pastor-parish relations committee chairperson. If it is with some leaders or members of the congregation, talk with your pastor and the church council. If you need to, talk with your district superintendent and get counsel.

● Read, go to appropriate workshops, and expand your field of view. Maybe you will see something fresh to open a doorway.

● Keep loving and praying. A lot is at stake around worship; if there are people with differing perspectives, they can become very restless and feisty. There is room at the table for all of you. You are a key leader in trying to get everyone to deal with diversity and to map out a way forward.

Discover Worship Resources

If worship is a new area of discovery and learning for you, you are in for a treat and a wonderful adventure. The books, magazines, Web sites, videos, and other resources available can be overwhelming. Don't lose heart! Take your time. Explore some basic resources. (See Resources) One good place to start is Hoyt Hickman's *United Methodist Worship*. Beyond that, be sure to spend some time reviewing *The United Methodist Book of Worship*, particularly its introductions to different sections. For example, see pages 13, 226, 238, 269, and 613.

Participate in Training Events

If you learn better in social situations, find out what training events, seminars, or workshops are available in your area. Most annual conferences and districts sponsor training opportunities related to worship. One thing you should not miss is the convocation of the Fellowship of United Methodists in Music and Worship Arts (FUMMWA). FUMMWA has a national convocation on the odd-numbered years and a jurisdictional gathering on the even-numbered years. These are wonderful opportunities for you and others (pastor, musicians, artists) to experience worship and to go to workshops on a wide range of topics, especially music, dance, and drama.

The Order of Saint Luke has a convocation every four years on some major worship topic and a retreat during the other three years. These gatherings are open to all interested persons.

See the Resources section beginning on page 28 for information on these organizations and other worship helps.

More Paths to Vital Worship

You will want to consider other long-range possibilities. Although these are not of such central importance as those we have already discussed, it is desirable that you or some person(s) in the congregation take responsibility for them. In all these responsibilities, cooperation with the pastor is essential. *Don't worry if you are unable to do all that is suggested below. The important thing is to have your priorities clear and to know where there is a need and to have the readiness to move ahead.*

The Study of Worship

Encourage and enable the study of worship by individuals and groups in your congregation. Work with your pastor and other leaders to develop a plan for educating your congregation in the meaning and practices of worship. See the materials recommended for this purpose in the Resources section.

Laypersons as Worship Leaders

Our understanding of worship as the work of God's people mandates that laypersons take an active role in worship planning and leadership. Traditional roles include ushers, greeters, acolytes, and the musical leaders. Laypersons increasingly are taking such leadership roles as reading Scripture, leading prayer, witnessing, sharing concerns of the church and world, and lay speaking—not only on special occasions, such as Laity Sunday but also on every Sunday. However, lay leadership will be effective only if lay leaders are adequately trained and prepared.

Furnishings, Paraments, and Sacramental Elements

There are in every congregation furnishings (altar table, pulpit/lectern, baptismal font, chairs and pews, and so forth); paraments (the seasonal colored cloths that cover the furnishings); and sacramental elements (water, bread, wine/grape juice, oil) for congregational worship that require ongoing attention and preparation. You may want to appoint groups, such as Communion stewards and an altar guild, to take these responsibilities. Such groups will find valuable help in the books *Worship Matters* (vol. 2) and *United Methodist Altars*, listed in the Resources section.

Multicultural Contributions

Your worship can take on new life as you enable the congregation to experience the worship style, music, art, and other contributions of various racial and ethnic groups. Doing so will not only honor and welcome persons from these cultural groups to your congregation but will also enrich your congregation's worship experience. Multicultural resources found in *The United Methodist Hymnal, The United Methodist Book of Worship,* and "How to Worship in Multicultural Congregations" by David Marcelo in *Worship Matters* (vol. 2) will be of value. *Mil Voces Para Celebrar* (our Spanish language hymnal/worshipbook), *Come, Let Us Worship* (our Korean-English bilingual hymnal/worshipbook), and *The Faith We Sing* are sources that you will want to use to expand congregational song. Additional multicultural music resources are listed in Resources.

Memorial Gifts for Worship

Many persons wish to give worship-related memorial gifts to their church, and it is important to have policies and controls to encourage needed gifts and prevent unwanted gifts. You or the worship group can take the lead in proposing a stated policy that prescribes a process for approving, placing, and using memorial gifts for worship. (The trustees generally oversee tangible gifts and memorial policies. You will want to consult with them.) This is not a matter of being ungrateful; it is a matter of ensuring that items added to the "holy things" used in worship are appropriate to the environment of worship in your worship space. If you need a model for such a statement, check with some of the larger churches in your area.

Arts Other Than Music

Worship that engages all the senses will include a wider use and understanding of the arts other than music—visual, dramatic, and architectural—as expressions of faith and means of proclaiming the gospel. Possibilities include banners, vestments, paraments, chrismons (ornamental symbols for hanging on the Christmas tree), drama, interpretive movement or sacred dance, artistic bulletin covers, projected graphics—the possibilities are limited only by the vision and gifts of your congregation. For further information, contact the Center for Worship Resourcing of the General Board of Discipleship. See also "The Role of Artists in Worship" by Sara Webb Phillips in *Worship Matters* (vol. 1) and "The Work of Visual Artists in Worship" by Ashley Calhoun in *Worship Matters* (vol. 2).

Architecture is crucial for worship because the design and setup of a room will determine the character of the worship experience. As your congregation evaluates the effectiveness of its worship space and makes decisions regarding possible changes, you and other leaders of the congregation need to see that the worship space enables, rather than hinders, worship. The book *Church Architecture: Building and Renovating for Christian Worship,* listed in Resources, is extremely valuable in guiding a congregation through such a building or renovation project.

For a resource to empower the congregation to be more sensitive and accessible to people with disabilities, secure *That All May Worship* (National Organization on Disability, 910 Sixteenth Street, NW, Suite 600, Washington DC 20006). 202-293-5960 or http://www.nod.org/publications. Click on "Religion and Disability Interfaith Guides."

What About Your Church Building?

The worship space of your church makes a powerful statement. Does it say what you believe God is trying to say to the people? Or does it contradict the gospel? What do people experience? Is the message of the room a call to awe and wonder? Or is the message a call to intimacy and shared experience? Does the room invite formality or informality? How do the arrangement of symbols, play of light, acoustics, accessibility, and visibility to the actions at pulpit, font, and table shape the people's experience of God?

A Worksheet for Planning a Worship Service

Here is a planning worksheet designed for worship using the calendar of the Christian year and the Revised Common Lectionary. It can be used or adapted for other approaches to worship. You are free to adapt it for your congregation's needs. You will need one sheet for each service you are planning.

A Worksheet for Planning a Worship Service

Date: _____

Day in the church year:

_____

Planning team:

_____

_____

Liturgical color: _____

Scripture readings:

First reading: _____

Psalm response: _____

Second reading: _____

Will there be Communion? _____

Baptism? _____

Special emphasis or special service?

_____

Gospel reading: _____

_____

Sermon focus: _____

_____

Hymns/songs:

_____ _____

_____ _____

_____ _____

_____ _____

_____ _____

_____ _____

_____ _____

_____ _____

Anthems:

_____ _____

_____ _____

Service/Communion music:

_____ _____

_____ _____

Instrumental music:

_____ _____

Assisting ministers/readers:

_____

_____

Acolytes:_____

_____

Other participants (actors, dancers, technicians, instrumentalists):

_____

_____

_____

Visuals:_____

_____

_____

Invitations to be made (commitment to discipleship, healing prayer):

_____

Other details for this service:

_____

_____

_____

Evaluation/Improvement:
• What worked well?
• What could be improved?
• In what ways? What did we learn?
• How will our learning be incorporated into next week's service?

Resources

The Center for Worship Resourcing, General Board of Discipleship.

• Weekly music, preaching, and worship planning helps:
www.umcworship.org.
• Music in churches with small membership; 877-899-2780, ext. 7073.
• Welcoming seekers and making disciples through worship; 877-899-2780,
ext. 7072.
• Preaching; 877-899-2780, ext. 7084.

Worship Reference Resources

• *By Water and the Spirit: A United Methodist Understanding of Baptism.*
Official statement on baptism. www.umcworship.org.

• *Come to the Waters,* by Daniel Benedict (Nashville: Discipleship
Resources, 1997 ISBN 0-88177-179-1). Proposes that churches take seri-
ously people's search for God and outlines a process for adult conversion.

• *Companion to The United Methodist Hymnal,* edited by Carlton Young
(Nashville: Abingdon Press, 1993 ISBN 0-687-09260-4). Offers background
on every hymn tune and text in *The United Methodist Hymnal* as well as
information regarding music in The United Methodist Church.

• *Contemporary Worship for the 21st Century: Worship or Evangelism?,* by
Daniel Benedict and Craig Kennet Miller (Nashville: Discipleship
Resources,1994 ISBN 0-88177-138-4). A resource for congregations seeking to expand the range of worship options within existing worship settings
or in adding worship services.

• *The Hymns of The United Methodist Hymnal,* edited by Diana Sanchez
(Nashville: Abingdon Press, 1989 ISBN 0-687-43149-2). Helps pastors,
musicians, and other leaders of worship to appreciate and use the hymns in
the hymnal and to discover fresh ways to sing and to accompany them.

• *This Holy Mystery: A United Methodist Understanding of Holy
Communion*—an official and comprehensive statement on the theology and
practice of Holy Communion. www.umcworship.org.

• *United Methodist Altars, Revised Edition,* by Hoyt L. Hickman (Nashville:
Abingdon Press, 1984, 1996 ISBN 0-0687-00562-0). A manual for all who
do the work of altar guilds and a resource for pastors and worship chairper-
sons.

• *United Methodist Worship,* by Hoyt L. Hickman (Nashville: Abingdon
Press, 1991. ISBN 0-687-43196-4). An introduction to United Methodist
worship for personal or group study.

• *Worship Matters: A United Methodist Guide to Ways of Worship,* vol. 1, edited by E. Byron Anderson (ISBN 0-88177-279-8), and *Worship Matters: A United Methodist Guide to Worship Work,* vol. 2, edited by E. Byron Anderson (ISBN 0-88177-280-1). (Nashville: Discipleship Resources, 1999.) Offer basic perspectives on worship in our tradition and help with practical issues for strengthening worship.

Hymnals, Books of Worship, and Liturgical Planning Resources

• *Come, Let Us Worship: The Korean-English Bilingual United Methodist Hymnal* (Nashville: United Methodist Publishing House, 2001 ISBN 0-687-08513-6).

• *The Faith We Sing* (Nashville: Abingdon Press, 2000. ISBN 0-687-09054-7). Contains a significant collection of new hymns, songs for praise and worship, global music, old favorites, for expanding the range of congregational song. Available in several editions: pew, accompaniment, simplified, choral, worship planner, guitar, audio, CD-ROM, MIDI, enlarged pew, hymn festival, compact disc accompaniment, presentation, Braille, American Sign Language.

• *Fiesta Christiana* (Nashville: Abingdon Press, 2003 ISBN 0-687-02159-6). Spanish language United Methodist book of worship.

• *Hymns and More,* a quarterly subscription service from Abingdon Press/Cokesbury, providing congregational hymns and songs, choruses, service music, and spoken acts of worship in a variety of musical styles, cultures and theological positions.

• *Hymns from the Four Winds* (Nashville: Abingdon Press, 1983 ISBN 0-687-18126-7). A collection of Asian American hymns.

• *Mil Voces Para Celebrar* (Nashville: Abingdon Press, 1996 ISBN 0-687-43183-2). The official Spanish language hymnal and worship book.

• *Program Calendar* (United Methodist Communications) (888) 862-3242. A helpful tool for planning worship in the context of the larger programs and ministries of the church. Lectionary readings are listed for each Sunday and special day.

• *Songs of Zion* (Nashville: Abingdon Press, 1981 ISBN 0-687-39120-2). A songbook from the African American religious tradition.

• *The United Methodist Book of Worship* (Nashville: United Methodist Publishing House, 1992). The official book of worship for planners and leaders of worship. This volume has resources for worship throughout the Christian year and for observances of special days.

• *The United Methodist Hymnal* (Nashville: United Methodist Publishing House, 1989). Our official hymnal.

• *The United Methodist Music and Worship Planner* (Nashville: Abingdon Press ISBN 04301-8). Published annually with lectionary readings printed in full text, suggested colors, hymns, anthems, contemporary, instrumental music and prayers.

Preaching Resources

• *Go Preach: A Primer for Beginning Preachers*, by John P. Gilbert (Nashville: Discipleship Resources, 2002 ISBN 0-88177-384-0).

• *Preaching the Revised Common Lectionary*, [Years A, B, C: 12 volumes] (Nashville: Abingdon Press, 1992, 1993, 1994).

• *The Revised Common Lectionary*, by the Consultation on Common Texts (Nashville: Abingdon Press, 1992 ISBN 0-687-36174-5).

Catalogs

Cokesbury Music Catalogs: Comprehensive Catalog of Resources for Music Ministry. Call 877-877-8674.

Organizations

Cokesbury Music Service, call 877-877-8674. Fax: 800-445-8189. Internet: www.cokesburymusic.com. Music service that allows ordering resources from most music publishers on one account.

The Fellowship of United Methodists in Music and Worship Arts, P.O. Box 24787, Nashville, TN 37202-4787. Call 800-952-8977, or toll 615-749-6875. Fax: 615-340-7006. E-mail: FUMMWA@aol.com. Web site www.fummwa.org. The fellowship is a membership organization providing resources and support for music and the arts in worship. The journal, *Worship Arts,* is published bimonthly. Membership includes professional and nonprofessional musicians, clergy, and persons interested in worship and the arts.

Methodist Musicians Listserv: a free, interactive Internet listserv for church musicians, pastors, worship planners and leaders, educators, and others interested in having discussion and information exchange on all matters related to United Methodist music and worship. To subscribe, send an email message to requests@lists.gbod.org. In the body of the email, include the following: subscribe MethodistMusicians.

National Organization on Disability, 910 Sixteenth Street NW, Suite 600, Washington, DC 20006. Call 202-293-5960.
Web site: www.nod.org/publications. Click on "Religion and Disability Interfaith Guides."

The Order of Saint Luke, P.O. Box 22279, Akron, OH 44302-0079. Telephone and fax: 330-535-8656. Web site: www.Saint-Luke.org. This is a community of people devoted to sacramental and liturgical scholarship, education, and practice. The order includes laypersons, seminarians, and clergy. It publishes *Sacramental Life* and *Doxology*. The order holds a retreat each year that is open to anyone interested in the retreat's theme.